BAR
CART
Style

BAR CART Style

CREATING SUPER-CHIC COCKTAIL STATIONS

Styled by
EMILY HENSON

RYLAND PETERS & SMALL
LONDON • NEW YORK

Senior Designer Toni Kay
Senior Commissioning Editor
 Annabel Morgan
Production Manager
 Gordana Simakovic
Art Director Leslie Harrington
Editorial Director Julia Charles
Publisher Cindy Richards
Stylist Emily Henson
Indexer Hilary Bird

First published in 2019
by Ryland Peters & Small
20–21 Jockey's Fields
London WC1R 4BW
and
341 E 116th St
New York NY 10029
www.rylandpeters.com

10 9 8 7 6 5 4 3 2

Original concept, design,
commissioned photography
and text by Emily Henson
copyright © Ryland Peters &
Small 2019. Recipe copyright
© Brontë Aurell, Julia Charles,
Jesse Estes, Laura Gladwin,
Ben Reed, David T. Smith
& Tristan Stephenson 2019.
See page 128 for full credits.

ISBN: 978 1 78879 160 1

A CIP record for this book is
available from the British Library.
Library of Congress Cataloging-
in-Publication data has been
applied for.

Printed in China

NOTES
• When using slices of citrus fruit
such as lemons or oranges in a
drink, try to find organic, unwaxed
fruits and wash well before using.
If you can only find treated fruit,
scrub well in warm soapy water
and rinse before using.
• Measurements are occasionally
given in barspoons, which are
equivalent to 5 ml or 1 teaspoon.

CONTENTS

INTRODUCTION

I'm not sure exactly who we have to thank for the comeback of the bar cart, but I for one am thrilled. The cocktail itself has been creeping back into the mainstream for some time now, with bartenders getting more and more inventive, sometimes insisting on putting on a show like Tom Cruise in the so-bad-it's-good 1980s film *Cocktail*. Now, every once in a while I love a night where I'm served the latest concoction by a bearded and tattooed bartender in a smart apron and bow tie, who insists I need to try the truffle-infused vodka or a Cacio e Pepe martini. But I'm also at that stage in life where I will complain about it, "It's so noisy, I can't hear my friends over the music, these drinks are so expensive, why is everyone so loud, when are we leaving…?" I'm definitely more of a homebody, but I do like to have fun and I love to have my friends over. So for those of us favouring a big night in over a big night out, creating cocktails at home is an appealing option. If it means I can entertain at home rather than brave London's often stifling, noisy and overpriced bar scene, then I'm sold.

Perhaps we also owe the recent interest in the home bar to romantic notions of bygone eras, fuelled by idealized versions represented in literature, TV and film. A certain television show comes to mind, set in 1960s New York, where scotch-swigging ad men have well-stocked bar carts both at home and at the office. Or maybe it's the perceived glamour of the Jazz Age, as epitomized in F. Scott Fitzgerald's *The Great Gatsby*, with Jay Gatsby hosting lavish cocktail-fuelled parties in his Long Island mansion. Whatever the inspiration, the bar cart is back and in styles to suit any home. If you're going to be impressing your guests – or even just your family – with your perfectly blended Old Fashioned or Singapore Sling, then you'll need to have a place for all the kit. Of course, you could stash your bottles and shakers in a kitchen cabinet, but it's so much more fun to make a statement and incorporate a stylish bar cart into your home.

On the following pages you'll find twelve ways to style a bar cart, each one as different and as inspiring as the next. You can replicate a look in full, or simply use one as a starting point for creating your very own style. Perhaps you'll see an idea that works with your current décor, or maybe you're so cocktail crazy that you'll feel inspired to re-style your living room around one of these designs! Alternatively, you may be hosting a themed party and want your bar cart to match the Mexican food or the Tiki style of the guests' costumes. With decorating and styling tips, as well as practical advice on all the cocktail-making accoutrements required to be the perfect host, this book will arm you with all that you need to build a bar cart with style.

THE COCKTAIL THROUGH TIME

THROUGHOUT THE 20TH CENTURY THE COCKTAIL WENT THROUGH BOOMS AND SLUMPS IN POPULARITY. IT ADAPTED TO SOCIAL PHENOMENA SUCH AS PROHIBITION, WAR, FREE LOVE, DRUG CULTURE, VARIOUS RISES AND FALLS OF THE STOCK MARKET AND THE POWER OF THE MEDIA, AND STILL FLOURISHES IN THE 21ST CENTURY, CONSTANTLY EVOLVING TO SUIT OUR THIRST FOR SOMETHING NEW AND DIFFERENT.

Although the golden age of cocktails probably fell between 1860 and 1920, it was arguably the roaring 1920s that saw cocktails come into their own. This happy time coincided with a most unhappy state of affairs in the USA – the social experiment called Prohibition (1920–1933). This era had a number of effects on drinking culture. It forced drinkers underground into illicit bars known as speakeasies. These bars weren't dives, though – quite the opposite; they were luxurious and lavishly decorated and much more female-friendly, which lent additional glamour to cocktails.

Because liquor was illegal, inferior bootleg (or moonshine) was drunk, but it was often so vile that bartenders would mix it with other juices and cordials to mask its aggressive flavour. Drinks created in these times had seemingly innocuous names designed to fool the authorities, and drinks would also be served in mugs in an effort to distract the hapless police force. Those bartenders who didn't wish to break the law during Prohibition hotfooted it to Europe or Cuba to ply their trade in a different country, but with as much enthusiasm as ever. This was a particularly creative time for them. Many of the drinks we count as classics today, from the Bloody Mary to the Sidecar, were invented overseas during that period, with the names of the bartenders who created them still hallowed in bars everywhere.

President Franklin D. Roosevelt had other ideas about Prohibition and it was repealed in 1933, not long after he came to office. An accomplished drinker and handy bartender himself, Roosevelt, along with Winston Churchill, was a great advocate of, among other cocktails, the martini. Indeed, it was during a summit meeting between Joseph Stalin, Churchill and Roosevelt in 1943 that

Roosevelt whipped up a round of Dirty Martinis for his companions. Perhaps the most iconic of all cocktails, this drink has been enjoyed and tinkered with by a greater alumni of politicians, playwrights and playboys than has ever gathered around a bar. And it was these legendary drinkers who made cocktails the stuff of blurred anecdote and folklore enshrined in times of glamour. Humphrey Bogart's dying words were reported to have been, "I should never have switched from Scotch to martinis" – perhaps not the most encouraging message for martini enthusiasts, but a fantastic quote nonetheless. Women, never much welcome in saloon bars, were greeted with open arms in the cocktail lounges of the 1930s. Although there were

still laws in place in some American states prohibiting women from ordering drinks at the bar, these were easily circumvented by implementing table service.

You may imagine that the 1940s bar was a place for reflection and austerity, mirroring the sombre post-war mood. Fortunately, a cocktail can be perfect for times of contemplation as well as jubilation. Soldiers returning from the South Pacific to America told tales of exotic Tiki cocktails made with rum and tropical fruit juices. Such tales prompted a cocktail menu trend that was championed by bartending legend Don the Beachcomber (he was of such high repute that his status was that usually afforded only to movie stars) and his pupil, Trader Vic. Zombies, mai tais and scorpions were all to become drinks that not only stood the test of time but also remind people of sun-kissed beaches and far flung holidays.

In the 1950s, cocktail culture moved to suburbia, becoming less formal. Amid mass migration out of the city and into the suburbs, America needed cocktails made for relaxing in the den before supper or entertaining at dinner parties. Women wore flowered cotton dresses, men Hawaiian shirts. Florida and California offered their own mid-century vision, centred on patios and swimming pools. But even though cocktail napkins were decorated with cute pictures and recipes, the napkins were still made of cloth. And men wouldn't dream of going tieless to a sophisticated cocktail lounge. The TV series *Mad Men* revived interest in this post work grown-up ritual. Whether at home or out before a commute, the cocktail hour usefully separated the workday from a presumably free evening.

The 1960s were, by and large, something of a non-starter when it came to cocktail consumption. Free love, drug culture and the perceived stuffiness of the 1950s cocktail lounge meant that cocktails didn't really move forward. And so to the next decade. Cocktails went the same way that most things went in the 1970s – take your pick, from the Tequila Sunrise to the Blue Hawaiian, the 1970s did to the cocktail what, well, the 1970s did to pretty much everything else! The 1980s didn't help the situation either. Spirits (and bank balances) were high, but never more so than when it came to the potency of cocktails. For some reason bartenders seemed to do their damnedest to stifle the creativity of cocktail making by performing such demeaning feats as stuffing Mars bars and jelly beans into bottles of vodka and selling them at irresponsibly cut prices.

The 1990s were definitely the years that saved the cocktail, with plenty to celebrate. This was the time when drinkers rediscovered high-potency, quality cocktails made with premium spirits and fresh fruits and juices. Bartenders started looking with interest towards the kitchen for fresh inspiration and new ingredients. And so it was, with the mantle of mixologist newly resurrected, that bartenders did their creative best to prove that pretty much anything is mixable. From fresh garlic and Lapsang Souchong tea to liquorice, basil, fennel and even Vimto, the mixologist had a point to prove.

By 2010, the bar industry had experienced an incredible decade of self-discovery, as classic cocktails were revived and new culinary techniques established themselves behind bars. Some of the practices, such as sous vide, have now found a permanent home in bar craft, others like hydrocolloid caviar pearls, have not. And, as we move to the end of another decade, the growing movement towards upcycling and low-environmental-impact food and drink has led many to rediscover traditional preparation and preservation practices, such as smoking and fermentation, and these techniques have broadened the flavour of cocktails enjoyed too. In addition, a new breed of non-alcoholic 'spirits' and mixers are taking the bar world by storm and opening up new avenues of alcohol-free mixology.

Who knows what lies in store for the cocktail? As long as people keep on enjoying mixed drinks and new and exciting spirits are unearthed around the globe, the world is our oyster. An aspect of cocktail creation is that cocktails are often more enjoyable when created yourself, whether for a group of friends or just for you after a hard day's graft. One thing is guaranteed – there is a cocktail for everyone and for every occasion; it's just down to you to experiment with some recipes and find it!

SETTING UP
A HOME BAR

BAR CART BASICS

Standard Spirits

Vodka – Absolut, Smirnoff

Gin – Gordon's, Beefeater

White rum – Havana Club 3 Year

Golden rum – Appleton Special, Bacardi Oro

Dark rum – Lamb's

Gold tequila – Cuervo Gold, Sauza Gold

Silver tequila – Sierra

Scotch whisky (blend) – Johnnie Walker Black

Bourbon whiskey – Jim Beam, Maker's Mark

Cognac – Hennessy Fine de Cognac

Luxury Spirits

Vodka – Belvedere, Grey Goose XV

Gin – Tanqueray No. Ten, Hendrick's

White rum – Trois Rivières Blanco

Aged rum – Bacardi 8, Facundo Exquisito

Dark rum – Gosling's

Aged tequila – Patron Gold Anejo, Sauza Conmemorativo

Scotch whisky – Johnnie Walker Blue

Bourbon whiskey – Woodford Reserve, Knob Creek

Cognac – Courvoisier XO Cognac

Liqueurs & Syrups

Orange-flavoured liqueurs – triple sec, Cointreau, curaçao (blue and/or clear)

Berry-flavoured liqueurs – crème de framboise, crème de cassis, crème de mûres, Chambord

Other fruit brandies and liqueurs – Archer's peach schnapps, Kuyper cherry brandy, Cherry Heering 200

Floral and botanical liqueurs – St-Germain (elderflower), crème de violette, Benedictine dom

Coffee- and chocolate-flavoured liqueurs – Tia Maria, Kalua, Crème de cacao

Almond-flavoured liqueur – Amaretto

Sugar syrup, Orgeat (almond syrup), cinnamon syrup

Fortified Wines & Aperitif Spirits

Vermouths – Martini Bianco, Martini Rosso, Antico Formula (aged)

Campari, Aperol

Dubonnet

Juices, Mixers & Seasonings

Freshly squeezed juices – lemon, lime

Other fruit juices – orange, cranberry, grapefruit, passion fruit

Assorted carbonated mixers – soda water, tonic water, lemonade, cola, ginger ale

Angostura bitters

Garnishes

Edgings – sugar, cocoa, salt

Lemons, limes, oranges, cherries, olives, cocktail onions

EQUIPMENT

FOR THE HOME BARTENDER, GETTING THE RIGHT EQUIPMENT CAN BE AS IMPORTANT AS THE TASTE OF THE FINAL DRINK ITSELF. YOU MAY FIND THAT YOU HAVE MOST OF WHAT YOU NEED IN YOUR OWN KITCHEN, BUT IF YOU WANT TO CREATE THE RIGHT ATMOSPHERE FOR YOUR GUESTS AND MIX COCKTAILS WITH FLAIR, IT'S WORTH INVESTING IN A FEW ACCESSORIES.

MEASURE OR JIGGER

The measure/jigger is an essential piece of equipment for making cocktails. Measures come in a variety of sizes, from the single shot of 25 ml/1 fl oz. to 175 ml/6 fl oz. for a glass of wine. Look for a handy inverted or double measure/jigger – one end holds 25 ml/1 fl oz., and the other 50 ml/2 fl oz.

SHAKER

The piece of kit most synonymous with the world of the 'spiritual advisor' is the cocktail shaker. While there are only two basic types of shaker – the three-piece (or deco) shaker and the Boston. The three-piece (so named as it comes in three pieces: the can, the strainer and the lid) is more suitable for home creations and for the more elegant world of the hotel bartender. Bartenders prefer the Boston shaker, purely for ergonomic reasons. Its two separate parts (the mixing glass and the can) allow the bartender more volume and yield greater results in the shake.

STRAINER

Whenever possible, strain your concoction over fresh ice, as the ice you have used in your shaker will have started to melt. If the Boston is your tool of choice, you will need something to strain the liquid out while keeping the ice in. There are two types of strainer – the Hawthorn strainer will sit happily over the metal part of the shaker, while the Julep fits in the mixing glass.

BARSPOON AND MUDDLER

The barspoon is the Swiss army penknife of the cocktail world. This tool comes in a number of styles; the long, spiral-stemmed, flat-bottomed spoon being the most versatile. As well as all the obvious uses for a spoon (measuring and stirring), the spiral stem and flat bottom allow its user to create layered drinks. The flat bottom can also be used for gentle muddling (dissolving powders into liquid, for example). If more labour-intensive muddling is required (such as extracting juice from fresh fruit) you may want a more

user-friendly piece of kit. The muddler and the imaginatively titled 'wood' or 'stick' are more ergonomic and won't cause you as much discomfort as a barspoon.

POURER

One of the tools that the professional bartender finds indispensable is the pourer (a thin stainless-steel spout mounted on a tapered plastic bung). This piece of kit allows the user to pour a liquid at a regulated rate. Bartenders count to a fixed number when pouring a spirit or liqueur to negate the use of a measure. Different liquors will pour at different speeds, however, depending on the amount of sugar in the liquid.

PAPER STRAWS

For anyone starting out in the world of cocktails, a straw is an essential tool. In the same way that a chef will taste a sauce before serving it, you will need to test the balance of your drink. Dip a straw into the beverage in question and once submerged place your finger over the top end to create a vacuum. Take the straw from the drink and suck the liquid from the straw – this small amount will be enough for you to determine whether your drink needs more sweetening or souring agent.

ICE BUCKET AND ICE TONGS

Ice is another essential tool for every bartender. Make sure you use mineral rather than tap water to fill your trays, to avoid chlorinated cubes. There are three different types of ice: cubed, crushed and shaved. Cubed ice will melt (and therefore add dilution) at a slower rate but will also chill a cocktail less effectively than crushed or shaved. Drinks using crushed ice have risen in popularity recently, owing to the arrival on the cocktail scene of concoctions like the Caipirinha and the Mojito. Shaved ice is mostly used in drinks that might require a little extra dilution to make them more palatable (remember, water is an important ingredient in a great many mixed drinks) and where they need to be as cold as possible.

Other useful accessories

KNIFE handy for preparing your garnishes.

JULEP STRAINER a stainless-steel strainer used when stirring a cocktail and pouring from the mixing glass. It is a versatile tool that can also be used as an alternative to the sieve.

SWIZZLE STICKS for stirring drinks that have been 'built' into the glass.

TEA STRAINER can be used if a cocktail needs to be fine-strained to extract unwanted ice chippings or the flesh or pips from fruit.

LEMON SQUEEZER for extracting the juices of citrus fruit.

BARTENDER'S FRIEND used for removing bottle tops and corks.

GLASSWARE

SHOT GLASS

A shot glass is fairly self-explanatory; it usually holds either a single or a double shot and is used to serve shots and shooters. It can also be used as a measure should you lose yours (a common occurrence even for the pros).

HEATPROOF GLASS

Take your pick from the wine-glass-shaped Irish coffee glass, to the sort of tall glass in which you might get served a café latte in a smart restaurant.

OLD-FASHIONED GLASS

Also known as the ROCKS GLASS or TUMBLER, this is used for drinks that are served on the rocks (short drinks over ice). It should have a capacity of about 300 ml/10 fl oz. and can also house drinks like whisky and soda.

WINE GLASSES

Classic small wine glasses are a good all-rounder and can be used for plenty of straight-up or punch-style drinks. Large balloon-shaped red wine glasses can work for Spanish-style Gin Tonica serves, in place of a currently fashionable gin copa/balon glass.

HIGHBALL GLASS

This is a tall, thin straight-sided glass used for long cocktails and also for serving spirits with mixers. Anything over 350 ml/12 fl oz. should suffice.

CHAMPAGNE FLUTE

As there is no real restriction on these, they can be as ornate as you choose.

MARTINI OR COCKTAIL GLASS

This is a small stemmed glass with an inverted cone bowl, mainly used to serve classic cocktails. The term cocktail glass is often used interchangeably with martini glass. The longer the stem, the more ornate. Anything between 150 ml/ 5 fl oz. and 200 ml/6 fl oz. should suffice for drinks that are served straight up.

HURRICANE GLASS

This multi-purpose glass comes in a number of different shapes and sizes. Generally seen as a glass that holds punches and frozen drinks, it is also known as the TULIP.

COUPE

Also used for classic straight-up cocktails, mini coupes have a shallow rounded bowl and a speak-easy, jazz-age elegance. A classic coupe has a large, shallow bowl and a longer stem. It can be used as an alternative to the flute for serving Champagne and works well for sparkling cocktails too.

TIKI MUG

These are novelty ceramic drinking vessels that originated in Tiki bars. They depict Polynesian or tropical themes, the most common being the Easter Island Moai statues. Despite being called mugs, they don't usually have a handle.

MARGARITA GLASS

This glass is also called the Marie Antoinette (so named as it is rumoured that the glass was shaped around the curve of her breast). A martini glass can also be used for a straight-up Margarita.

TANKARD

Often made from hammered copper, these handled cups are classically used to serve the Moscow Mule. Also, a traditional 'purl' tankard (made from pewter or stainless steel) was used to serve the earliest hot drinks the purl or flip, where a hot poker was plunged into the liquid in the cup to heat it through.

TECHNIQUES

THERE ARE BASIC TECHNIQUES BEHIND THE CREATION OF A COCKTAIL –
LAYERING, BUILDING, STIRRING, MUDDLING, SHAKING AND BLENDING.
WHEN CREATING A MIXED DRINK, THERE ARE TWO IMPORTANT PRINCIPLES
– FIRST, TO MARRY THE FLAVOURS OF THE INGREDIENTS AND SECONDLY,
TO CHILL THEM. THESE SIMPLE PRINCIPLES CAN BE APPLIED TO VIRTUALLY
ANY MIXED DRINK (WITH THE EXCEPTION OF LAYERED DRINKS).

BUILDING

This is the process used to describe
pouring a drink into a glass, one ingredient
after another. It is the technique you would
use to make a tall drink such as a gin and
tonic or a Screwdriver. When building a
drink, always add as much ice to the glass
as possible. Once built in the glass, the
mixture may require a quick stir with a
barspoon or the addition of a swizzle stick.

STIRRING

When the ingredients in a drink are all
alcoholic, the best method of mixing and
chilling them is stirring. Stirred drinks should
always be made in the mixing glass. If you
have time, chill the glass first by adding ice
and stirring gently with a barspoon (make
sure any dilution is discarded before the
alcohol is added), or place the glass in
the freezer for an hour prior to making
the drink. When stirring a drink, place the
spoon in the glass and gently stir the ice

in a continuous manner. Add all of the ingredients and continue stirring until the liquid is as cold as it can be (about 0°C/32°F). You may find it easier to strain the drink from the mixing glass using a Julep strainer.

MUDDLING

Muddling a drink may require the use of a barspoon, a muddler or a stick, depending on the intensity of the muddling. As opposed to a stirred drink, a muddled drink will invariably incorporate the intentional dilution of ice at some stage. Whether releasing the flavour or aroma of a herb, such as mint in the Mojito, extracting the juices from a fruit, such as fresh limes in a Caipirinha, or dissolving powder into a liquid, such as sugar into an Old Fashioned, the tool may change but the method remains the same.

BLENDING

You would usually be called upon to blend a drink when its ingredients involve heavy dairy products (as in the Piña Colada) or fresh fruit and frozen variations on classic drinks (strawberry daiquiris or frozen margaritas). Always use crushed ice in a blender and blend for about 20 seconds. When adding the crushed ice, less is more. Add too much ice and the drink becomes solid in constitution. Add a little at a time, though, and you can achieve the perfect thickness. Blending a cocktail will invariably produce an ultra-cold, thirst-quenching cocktail. As the ice is crushed, the drink

will dilute or separate quite quickly, though. Be warned: no one likes a slushy cocktail.

SHAKING

Drinks that contain 'heavy' ingredients require a more aggressive method of mixing and chilling. You will find that a good, sharp shake will bring life to heavy ingredients. When shaking a cocktail, there are a few things to remember. Whether you are using a three-piece or a Boston, make sure you have one hand at each end of the shaker and shake vertically, allowing the ice and liquid to travel the full distance of the shaker. When using a Boston shaker, the cocktail should always be made in the mixing glass, so those who are enjoying the spectacle of your labour can see what is going into the drink. Add as much ice to the mixing glass as possible and attach the can squarely over the top to create a vacuum. Shake sharply until the outside of the stainless-steel part of the shaker frosts over. Next, hold the can firmly in one hand and, using the heel of your other hand, hit the top of the can's rim to break the vacuum and remove the mixing glass. Always pour from the metal part of the shaker (it has a lip to stop the liquid dribbling down the outside of the vessel, and the metal will help to sustain the temperature of the drink). Finally, place a Hawthorn strainer on top of the can. Hold the top of the strainer with your middle finger, grasp the can with your other fingers and strain slowly into the glass.

THE CARTS

JAZZ AGE

JAZZ AGE

WHEN PROHIBITION WAS INTRODUCED IN THE US IN 1920, IT GAVE RISE TO THE ILLICIT DRINKING DEN KNOWN AS THE SPEAKEASY AND THE JAZZ MUSIC THAT BECAME SYNONYMOUS WITH THAT ERA.

In dimly lit rooms, drunken revellers danced with flailing arms and legs, enjoying the bootleg spirits all the more because they were forbidden. By no means are you required to flail your arms, but why not create your own secret speakeasy – in a corner of your living room perhaps? Darker settings create the right vibe, so wallpaper, dark paint or brick all make the perfect backdrop. Start with a decadent bar cart in gold or silver, perhaps with marble or mirrored shelves. Add a selection of delicate Champagne coupes – maybe vintage finds – and some dainty bar accessories like glass straws and beaded coasters. Muted lighting is essential for creating the mood, so dim the overheads and add some candlesticks in with your bottles. For a nod to the jazz age, look out for vintage musical instruments to use as props. And finally a disco ball, for a cheeky modern twist.

ABOVE **Secret passwords and hidden doors are not required here, just dainty coupes and opulent coasters to strike a note of jazz-age elegance.**

OPPOSITE **This bijou cart evokes all the glamour of the Gatsby era. It's perfect for smaller spaces and the marble and gilt finish adds a touch of luxe to proceedings.**

RIGHT Now that we all know that plastic straws are a no-no, have some fun sourcing reusable straws to use in their place. These delicate glass drinking straws featuring gold animal charms are sure to be a talking point, but gold-coloured metal straws would also work well on this cart.

LEFT Collecting accessories for a cart can be a lot of fun. These tiny hand-painted glasses were a lucky car boot/yard sale find, while the gleaming brass jigger plays both a decorative and practical role. Beaded coasters bring a hint of flapper styling, as do the glass straws.

OPPOSITE Cocktails became increasingly popular during Prohibition, not least because added ingredients such as cordials and liqueurs made bathtub gin more palatable. Look out for unusual examples when you're on your travels.

Aviation Royale

Channel the 1920s Jazz Age with this sparkling variation on the classic Aviation cocktail. It's based on a sophisticated combination of gin and maraschino cherry liqueur, with a splash of crème de violette for its perfume. Choose small vintage Champagne coupes to serve this intriguing cocktail in roaring 20s style!

25 ml/1 fl oz. gin (Tanqueray)

10 ml/⅓ fl oz. freshly squeezed lemon juice

1½ teaspoons maraschino liqueur (Luxardo)

dash of crème de violette

well-chilled Champagne, to top up

maraschino cherry, to garnish

cocktail shaker

stainless-steel cocktail stick

Champagne coupe

SERVES 1

Pour the first four ingredients into an ice-filled cocktail shaker and stir well. Strain into a chilled Champagne coupe and top up with Champagne. Garnish with a maraschino cherry on a stainless-steel cocktail stick and serve.

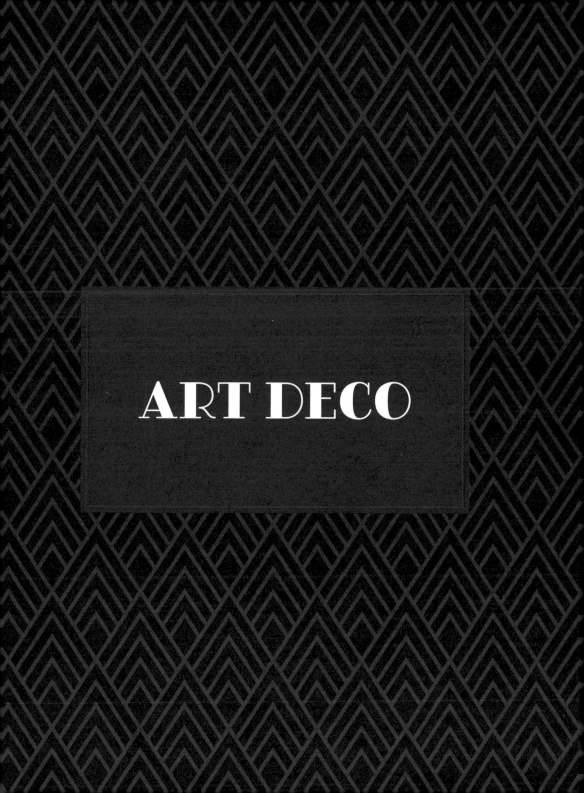

ART DECO

ART DECO

NOTHING CONJURES A SPIRIT OF MODERNITY AND GLAMOUR QUITE LIKE THE ART DECO ERA, WITH ITS STREAMLINED SHAPES, GLEAMING METALLICS AND LUXE FINISHES.

Creating an Art Deco-inspired bar at home may seem a challenge, but invest in a knockout cart and you're already halfway there. Metal finishes and symmetrical shapes are typical of the look, so something circular and gold is the way to go, although you could opt for a matte finish for a more modern look. A striking wallpapered backdrop will give this cart a boost, although a large framed painting or oversized mirror will create a similar effect. When it comes to stocking the cart, stick to gold barware and introduce black accents in your accessories, like coasters and stirrers. A tray is useful for corralling loose barware, but also for serving drinks. Limit your glassware to coupes, perhaps pink-tinted or gold-rimmed, and flutes, suited to both Champagne and Champagne cocktails.

ABOVE Gold accents work perfectly with this cart, and the woven-effect glass shaker strikes just the right note of glamour and opulence.

OPPOSITE Art Deco style is characterized by geometric shapes, bold detailing and luxurious finishes. This circular cart conjures up the radiating sunburst motif so typical of the era and has a suitably polished, high-shine finish.

LEFT An Art Deco cart is the perfect excuse for all manner of glamorous cocktail paraphernalia, from elegant barspoons to gold inlaid coasters.

BELOW When it comes to choosing liqueurs, look for those with interesting bottles in keeping with your theme.

OPPOSITE A classic Champagne coupe or saucer is surely the most elegant of all cocktail glasses. They're ideal for Champagne cocktails, of course, but they also work well for straight-up drinks. Gold-rimmed versions like these ones channel the glamour of the Art Deco age.

Blackberry Bellini

A classic Bellini is peach purée with Prosecco but the sour-sweetness of ripe blackberries works beautifully here to create a darkly elegant drink in keeping with the Art Deco Style. Champagne flutes embody the luxurious feel of the Art Deco movement and the deep purple colour of this cocktail will stand out against your gleaming gold barware.

4 fresh blackberries, plus 1 extra, to garnish

1 teaspoon caster/ granulated sugar

30 ml/1 fl oz. gin (Tanqueray No. Ten)

2 teaspoons freshly squeezed lemon juice

well-chilled Cremant or Champagne, to top up

cocktail shaker

muddler (optional)

stainless-steel cocktail stick

Champagne flute

SERVES 1

Put the 4 blackberries and sugar in a cocktail shaker and gently muddle with a muddler or handle of a rolling pin.

Add some ice cubes, the gin and lemon juice to the shaker and shake until cold, about 20 seconds. Strain into a Champagne flute, top up with cold Cremant or Champagne and garnish with a blackberry on a stainless-steel cocktail stick. Serve at once.

PALM SPRINGS

PALM SPRINGS

EVEN IF YOU DON'T HAVE FABULOUSLY BOLD GEOMETRIC WALLPAPER, YOU
CAN STILL CREATE A SLICE OF PLAYFUL, SUNNY PALM SPRINGS STYLE AT HOME.

The trick to nailing this look is finding the
right balance between glamour and kitsch.
By using warm metallics – in this case brass
and gold – your bar cart will ooze Southern
Californian poolside-chic. Scour junk shops
or antique markets for gold-rimmed and
decorated glassware in various shapes and
sizes. Tall ones for long drinks, dainty liqueur
glasses for an after-dinner chaser and small
bowls for garnishes or salty snacks. For a
tongue-in-cheek element, add a pop of
colour in a shiny finish, like a yellow bowling
ball ice bucket. By hanging a painting above
your cart and bringing in complementary
home accessories, you can create a striking
colour story that links the cart to the rest of
your home. Finish the look with a glass vase
of dried desert flowers or a potted cactus.

OPPOSITE AND RIGHT **Commitment to**
a colour scheme brings visual impact. Here,
brass detailing on the cart is echoed in the
buttercup yellow of the glossy acrylic ice
bucket and the quirky retro-style vase.

ABOVE LEFT AND RIGHT Gold-rimmed glasses bring a festive note whatever you're serving. Ebay is a great source of vintage glassware, but if you don't have time to stalk online auctions try Etsy for other vintage pieces or look for pretty modern glassware – there's plenty of it around. Decorative glasses are a must on any bar cart, just make sure they're in keeping with your decorative theme and the drinks you plan to serve.

ABOVE LEFT AND RIGHT Dressing up your cart with something living keeps it fresh and interesting. Suitable garnishes are the obvious choice – here limes and passion fruit – but a vase of flowers brings height to a cart and stops the overall look from becoming too blocky. It's also fun to add a 'wow' piece that grabs the eye, such as this vintage 1970s yellow ice bucket from vitrine3.com.

Beachcomber's Gold

This deliciously refreshing punch was originally served in an ice shell, made by pressing crushed ice into a glass until it rises up over the sides. Serve at home in elegant tumblers and add a glass cocktail stirrer to each for a little Palm Springs glamour.

200 ml/¾ cup honey

150 ml/⅔ cup fresh lime juice (about 5 limes)

250 ml/1 cup light Cuban-style rum (Bacardi)

250 ml/1 cup dark Jamaican rum (Captain Morgan)

500 ml/2 cups passion fruit juice

1 teaspoon Angostura bitters

passion fruit wedges, to garnish

glass punch jug/pitcher

barspoon or stirrer

tumblers or rocks glasses

SERVES 10

Put the honey and lime juice in a jug/pitcher and stir until the honey has dissolved. Add the remaining ingredients and some crushed ice and stir gently to mix. Serve in ice-filled glasses garnished with wedges of passion fruit.

MID-CENTURY

MID-CENTURY

IF YOU'VE EVER WATCHED AN EPISODE OF *MAD MEN*, YOU MAY HAVE FELT AN IRRESISTIBLE URGE TO POUR YOURSELF A STIFF DRINK.

The characters seem to drink morning, noon and night, somehow managing to come up with savvy ad campaigns at the same time. I'm not advocating that you have a shot of vodka with your cornflakes, but may I suggest a cart inspired by New York in the 1950s? This retro bar cart lends itself to a more traditionally masculine environment – clean lines, solid shapes, not too much fuss. If you can, get your hands on a wooden cart – perhaps teak and polished chrome. Search online for an original or look for a reproduction. There's no need to have too many shapes and sizes of glass. A nice selection of Old Fashioned tumblers is really all you'll need. Cut crystal examples with heavy bottoms and silver rims would be perfect. A mixing glass, an elegant metal stirrer and a strainer are all that's necessary to concoct the perfect Old Fashioned, but keep a shaker on standby for those early morning martinis.

ABOVE Masculine accessories with uncluttered lines work brilliantly with this cart. This wooden candlestick has been repurposed as a holder for metal stirrers.

OPPOSITE This 1950s cart boasts sleek formica surfaces and a built-in bottle rack. Look for something similar at car boot/yard sales or seek out modern reproductions.

OPPOSITE Thanks to the mass production techniques of the 1950s, it's still relatively easy to find complete original glassware sets and a retro-style bar cart is the perfect place to show off your finds.

ABOVE LEFT AND RIGHT Heavy glassware brings a luxe feel. Have some fun sourcing vintage pieces, and if you only find one survivor from a matching set, use it to hold stirrers, a muddler or tongs. An ice bucket is a must-have – we chose a vintage cut-glass example, but a sturdy mid-century or Danish Modern bucket would work perfectly, as would a chrome version to pick up the cart's detailing.

Old Fashioned

One of the most popular cocktails of all time, this drink is likely the 'original cocktail' – in the sense that the oldest recorded recipe we have for a cocktail lists the ingredients as a base spirit, bitters, sugar and water (or ice). The Old Fashioned has come back in vogue in recent years, thanks to the influence of the *Mad Men* TV series. An elegant cut-glass rocks glass is the only way to serve this classic.

1½ teaspoons Demerara/turbinado sugar syrup

3 dashes of Angostura bitters

60 ml/2 fl oz. bourbon (Michter's)

large strip of orange zest, to garnish

mixing glass or cocktail shaker

barspoon or stirrer

rocks glass

SERVES 1

Combine all the drink ingredients in a mixing glass or cocktail shaker with a large scoop of cubed ice and stir for 20–30 seconds. Strain into a rocks glass over cubed ice. Squeeze the orange zest over the top of the drink to express the citrus oils, then drop into the glass to garnish.

TROPICAL TIKI

TROPICAL TIKI

FOR THE RUM LOVER, WHAT BETTER WAY TO CELEBRATE YOUR FAVOURITE TIPPLE THAN WITH A TROPICAL TIKI-INSPIRED BAR CART AT HOME?

This isn't a theme you can take halfway – in fact, it's a great excuse to let loose and be just a little bit tacky. The more kitsch the better! Start with a cart in a warm metallic finish or fashioned from bamboo or rattan/wicker. Begin to layer in vibrant glassware in shapes and sizes that can accommodate cocktails with a long list of ingredients, not to mention plenty of ice. Add ceramic mugs in classic Tiki styles – totems, conch shells, toucans, monkeys… It's a great excuse to start a new collection. For parties you could even serve drinks in hollowed-out pineapples, using the fruit's flesh as garnish. Make sure to have a stash of novelty swizzle sticks topped with flamingos and palm trees – preferably glass, but if you must use plastic, re-use rather than throw away. And of course, paper umbrellas to top off each drink.

ABOVE AND OPPOSITE There are a few key ingredients for a successful Tiki cart. Look for glassware and decorative accessories with a colourful, tropical vibe. Bamboo detailing, wooden masks and carvings and luaus bring to mind all things Polynesian.

OPPOSITE If you're a rum lover, this is the cart for you. Tiki cocktails usually combine the spirit with mixers including fresh juices and spicy flavours, but artisanal rums are increasingly popular and can be sipped neat from a small glass.

ABOVE Tiki cocktails are the perfect excuse to break out the kitsch accessories, such as cocktail umbrellas and anything decorated with hula girls, pineapples or pink flamingos.

LEFT Novelty Tiki mugs make a fun addition to your glassware collection and are the perfect way to serve up a Zombie, Mai Tai or Navy Grog. They're available in a huge range of colours, shapes and sizes and depict typical Polynesian themes, from coconuts to Easter Island heads.

Mai Tai

No tropical Tiki bar cart would be complete without stocking the ingredients to make this famous drink. The Mai Tai is the flagship cocktail of the Tiki movement – a Polynesian theme that began in the 1930s and is still popular today thanks to its kitsch appeal. You will see this drink made in a hundred different ways in bars around the world, but this is Trader Vic's original recipe.

500 ml/2 cups dark Jamaican rum (Captain Morgan)

300 ml/1¼ cups freshly squeezed lime juice (about 10 limes)

150 ml/²⁄₃ cup orange curaçao

150 ml/²⁄₃ cup orgeat syrup (Monin)

scant 50 ml/¼ cup sugar syrup

pineapple slices and fresh mint sprigs, to garnish

large punch bowl

barspoon or stirrer

Tiki mugs or glass tumblers

SERVES 10

Pour all the ingredients into a large punch bowl filled with ice and stir gently to mix. Serve in ice-filled Tiki mugs (if you have them) or glass tumblers, garnished with pineapple slices and mint sprigs.

COLONIAL CHIC

COLONIAL CHIC

TO CREATE A SENSE OF A WARM AND
BREEZY FAR-FLUNG DESTINATION, DESIGN
YOURSELF A DAZZLING BAR FILLED WITH
GLEAMING GOLDS AND EXOTIC PATTERN.

Begin with a bar cart in an ornate design – perhaps
with metal legs shaped like bamboo or rope. A rattan
cart would work equally well. If you opt for metal,
adding seagrass mats gives texture and warmth.
This striking wallpaper really sets the tone, but for
a less permanent option, position your bar near a
window and hang a patterned curtain as a backdrop.
Adding a vase of colourful flowers to the top shelf of
your cart also introduces a jolt of colour. Sticking to
a colour palette – here blue, yellow and gold – helps
unify a look. Whatever you choose, limit yourself to
three or four colours when picking textiles, ceramics
and glassware. Finish with barware in bamboo and
tinted glass and a patterned bowl for garnishes
to tie the colours together. Now take a seat, sip
a Singapore sling and imagine you're surveying
the scene from the verandah at Raffles Hotel.

OPPOSITE AND RIGHT You'll probably want to style a bar cart to work with your existing
décor. The showstopping blue wallpaper here dictated a blue colour scheme with metallic
highlights and a yellow accent colour in the shape of a fruit bowl and glassware. A coherent
colour palette makes a cart look polished and professional.

ABOVE LEFT When it comes to dressing your cart, fresh flowers are the perfect decorative accessory, as is a leafy green plant or a candlestick or two.

ABOVE RIGHT Gin was the chosen spirit of the British Empire during the colonial era. Tonic water contained high levels of quinine, which prevented malaria, but was bitter and harsh. Colonial settlers mixed it with gin, lemon, sugar and ice to make it more palatable.

ABOVE LEFT If you don't have space for a vase of flowers, add a bowl of lemons and limes and have a chopping board and sharp knife at the ready. Keep mixers in the fridge till the last minute and remember to fill up your ice tray in advance.

ABOVE RIGHT Have some fun with quirky decorative accessories – glass stirrers and straws, swizzle sticks and unusual cocktail equipment all add personality and interest.

Singapore Sling

Best served from your bar cart on a balmy summer's evening, this gin-based cocktail couldn't be more at home within colonial chic styling. The story goes that it was developed in 1915 by bartender Ngiam Tong Boon at the luxurious Raffles Hotel in Singapore, which is named after the colonial founder of Singapore, Sir Stamford Raffles. This long, refreshing drink was a favourite of ex-pats back then, and is recognized as a classic around the world now.

35 ml/1¼ fl oz. gin (Tanqueray)

15 ml/½ fl oz. cherry liqueur (Heering)

1 teaspoon Benedictine D.O.M liqueur

15 ml/½ fl oz. freshly squeezed lemon juice

2 dashes of Angostura bitters

splash of soda water, to top up

lemon slice, to garnish

barspoon or stirrer

highball or sling glass

SERVES 1

Build the ingredients into a chilled highball (or sling) glass filled with cubed ice, then give it a quick stir and top with a splash of soda water. Garnish with a lemon slice.

MEXICAN FIESTA

MEXICAN FIESTA

WHETHER YOUR HOME IS ALREADY BOLDLY DECORATED OR YOU JUST WANT TO SPICE THINGS UP FOR A PARTY, THIS IS A QUICK AND EASY LOOK TO PULL TOGETHER.

The blue wall and red cabinet definitely make this look pop, but if you don't fancy painting a wall try hanging a length of vibrant fabric. Using the top of a dresser or low cabinet is a creative way to build a bar cart without an actual cart, the only downside being that it isn't mobile. A brightly painted canvas sets the colour scheme and is echoed in the plastic basket and *papel picado* (that's paper banner to you and me). Seek out handblown glassware with coloured rims, particularly cobalt blue, choosing large stemmed bowls for margaritas and shot glasses for straight tequila. A painted ceramic jug/pitcher adds character and can moonlight as a flower vase when not in use. Use decorative Mexican tiles as coasters and round out the look with novelty stirrers, more sophisticated in glass rather than plastic.

ABOVE AND OPPOSITE Bursting with colour, this cart is perfect for a summer party and is easy and inexpensive to put together. Look for artisanal pottery, such as a folksy ceramic mixing jug/pitcher or fruit bowl, and chunky glassware in jewel shades. It's also easy to set up out of doors if you're entertaining alfresco.

LEFT Decorative *papel picado* designs add an exuberant fiesta vibe. These paper flags and banners are used to decorate buildings, altars and streets during secular and religious celebrations in Mexico. Etsy has a great selection. You could even add a piñata if you want to liven things up a little.

BELOW For a truly authentic experience, do as the Mexicans do – sip your tequila neat from the freezer and choose 100% agave tequila to supposedly escape a hangover.

OPPOSITE Spruce up your cart with sturdy recycled handblown glassware from Mexico – it's both decorative and functional. The vivid cobalt shade is typical of the region, while the cute glass cactus stirrer continues the theme.

Jalisco Flower

A Mexican Fiesta themed cart needs to offer drinks that will live up to its vibrant colours and promise of a good time. Lovers of tequila will be wowed by this classy, slightly unusual combination of tequila, elderflower, grapefruit juice and Cava. The edible flower garnish adds yet another colourful touch and the margarita glasses for serving are a given. Arriba!

15 ml/½ fl oz. tequila blanco (Olmeca)

20 ml/¾ fl oz. elderflower liqueur (St-Germain)

35 ml/1¼ fl oz. pink grapefruit juice

well-chilled Prosecco or Cava, to top up

edible flower, such as nasturtium or violet, to garnish

cocktail shaker

barspoon or stirrer

margarita glass

SERVES 1

Put the tequila, elderflower liqueur and pink grapefruit juice in a cocktail shaker and add a handful of ice cubes. Shake well and strain into a chilled margarita glass. Top up with Prosecco or Cava and garnish with an edible flower.

GIN PALACE

GIN PALACE

IN RECENT YEARS GIN HAS MADE SOMETHING OF A COMEBACK, WITH
SMALL BATCH DISTILLERIES EXPERIMENTING WITH FRESH COMBINATIONS
OF BOTANICALS AND INGREDIENTS LIKE ROSE PETALS AND TRUFFLES.

However, the drink has had a somewhat chequered
history. During the first half of the 18th century,
it contributed to the ruin of many working class
Londoners, it was drunk by children in slums, and
even turned people blind (that might have been
the sulphuric acid sometimes added to make it taste
'better'). By the middle of the 19th century, stricter
regulation meant gin was less toxic and gin palaces
began to appear – stylishly decorated bars that
sparkled by gaslight. To style your own gin palace,
start with a bar cart with vintage flair. Prop an
upholstered screen behind (or a framed piece
of fabric or wallpaper, perhaps a William Morris
design). Have fun with glassware, choosing etched
or cut glass designs in a variety of sizes for all
manner of gin cocktails. Add a silver tray, a vintage
ice bucket and a cocktail shaker and you're all
ready for some mother's ruin!

OPPOSITE AND RIGHT With its elegant shape and
delicate filigree edging, this cart may look antique
but it's actually modern. Try flea markets or ebay
for a vintage example.

OPPOSITE There are so many classic gin-based cocktails that it could be argued that no bar cart is complete without a bottle of this versatile juniper-based spirit. The current craze for interesting gins made by small scale producers has led to a plethora of fabulous new bottle and label designs, which make the perfect addition to any gin lover's cart.

ABOVE LEFT Trays are a great addition to any cart. They can hold garnishes or ingredients, corral together matching sets of glassware and come in handy when you're handing around drinks.

ABOVE RIGHT If it's a special occasion, put a bottle of bubbles on ice for a classic gin and fizz cocktail such as the supremely chic French 75. The vintage ice bucket is from vitrine3.com.

Barrel-aged G&T

Gin is typically thought of as unaged, but increasingly distillers are experimenting with barrel-aged versions, like the one used here. If you are going to name a corner of your living room a Gin Palace, put down the basic gins and instead stock up on artisanal tipples like this one. These Spanish-style copa serving glasses are ideally shaped to let you appreciate the flavours of a wonderful gin, but of course highball glasses are fine too.

50 ml/2 fl oz. gin (Two Birds Sipping Gin)

120 ml/4 fl oz. tonic water (Fentimans 19:05)

fresh blackberries, to garnish

gin copa glass

stainless-steel cocktail stick

barspoon or stirrer

SERVES 1

Add ice cubes to fill ¾ of the glass. Stir gently for 15 seconds with a barspoon to chill the glass. Pour away any liquid from the melted ice. Top up the glass with more ice. Add the gin, trying to ensure that you coat the ice as you pour. Add the tonic water. Pouring slowly helps the tonic to keep its fizz. Add your garnish of blackberries on a stainless-steel cocktail stick. Let rest for 30 seconds to allow the flavours to integrate before serving.

DOLCE VITA

DOLCE VITA

IF YOU'VE EVER FANCIED YOURSELF AS THE STAR OF A FELLINI FILM, FROLICKING IN A ROMAN FOUNTAIN, THEN YOU'LL NEED THE APPROPRIATE DRINK TO FUEL THE FANTASY.

For classic Italian cocktails only a few key ingredients are required, so a compact cart is all you'll need. Choose something brass, mirrored and angular for the full *La Dolce Vita* effect. Treat your guests (or yourself) to an *aperitivo*, a pre-dinner drink to whet your appetite, usually accompanied by a small salty snack. The classic Negroni is a wonderful place to start and a solid chunky tumbler works best. Opt for a simple thick-bottomed, straight-sided style or something with a little more flair such as cut crystal or reeded sides. For a post-dinner *digestivo*, be sure to also have liqueur or shot glasses from which to enjoy that special bottle of Amaro you pick up in Rome. A mini ice bucket, a small dish for orange slices and a jug/pitcher for a refreshing round of Aperol Spritzes will finish things off nicely. Salute!

OPPOSITE AND LEFT Take inspiration from your travels and theme a cart around a particular country or city. This cart draws inspiration from the Italy of the 1950s and 60s, giving the opportunity to indulge in some retro Italian styling.

ABOVE LEFT AND RIGHT One of the many civilized habits of Italian daily life
is the *aperitivo* – a typically rather bitter pre-dinner drink enjoyed among friends
alongside some salty snacks. Typical *aperitivos* include Campari, vermouth,
a negroni or a spritz – a blend of a bitter liqueur, Prosecco and fizzy water.

ABOVE LEFT AND RIGHT There are a few essential accessories for this cart. A soda siphon is the perfect addition if you're a spritz fan – look on ebay for vintage examples. You'll need an ice bucket if you're serving Campari sodas, negronis or vermouth on the rocks – this is a vintage French one, but it fits well with the colour scheme. And when it comes to glassware, look for retro styles like these chunky pressed-glass tumblers – in keeping with the 1960s vibe.

Negroni

An obvious choice for a Dolce Vita theme is the Italian king of aperitivo cocktails, the Negroni. Bracingly strong, moreishly bitter and wonderfully easy to make, they are certainly a worthy component of the good life. New initiates could choose to start with Aperol instead of Campari – it's like Campari's better natured, more easy-going cousin. If the bitterness is still too much you can always drop the ratio slightly, or alternatively up the gin...

**25 ml/1 fl oz. gin
(avoid citrus-forward gins
as they get lost)**

25 ml/1 fl oz. Campari

**25 ml/1 fl oz. vermouth
(Nardini Rosso)**

**strip of grapefruit zest
or orange slice, to garnish**

rocks glass

barspoon or stirrer

SERVES 1

Build the drink ingredients in a rocks glass over ice. Stir for a full minute, then garnish with a small strip of grapefruit zest or an orange slice.

AFTER
DARK

AFTER DARK

THERE'S SOMETHING VERY GROWN UP ABOUT HAVING AN AFTER-DINNER DRINK AT HOME. WHEN DINNER GUESTS JOIN YOU, IT'S EVEN BETTER.

Having a bar stocked with various digestifs is a welcome end to any dinner party, or a more sophisticated way to keep the party going than dashing to the corner shop for another bottle of cheap wine. It's also a good excuse for picking up a bottle of whatever the locals drink whenever you travel. Create a mood that will make your guests want to linger – dark walls and low lighting to make your glasses sparkle by candlelight. Vintage glasses are the way to go, if you can find them. Look out for tiny liqueur glasses at charity/thrift shops or car boot/yard sales and build a charmingly mismatched collection. Adding a low-hanging pendant light above or close to your bar cart will help illuminate the drink pouring and the shimmering light will add an element of intimacy to proceedings. Finish with a vase of fresh flowers and bowl of maraschino cherries for a retro nod.

ABOVE When it comes to stocking the cart, look for dainty, small-scale glassware, as after-dinner drinks are generally quite high in alcohol and should be sipped rather than swigged. Cordial glasses are perfect, as are small coupes and dessert wine glasses.

OPPOSITE This elegant vintage-style cart is actually a modern design from Graham & Green. Amp up the after-dark vibe by choosing lighting that creates an intimate effect. This decadent fringed shade is by Anna Hayman.

OPPOSITE An after-dinner cart offers the opportunity to go a little bit old-school and indulge in a few pretty, retro bottles. Who can resist the old-fashioned charm of cherry brandy, Tia Maria and Cointreau?

ABOVE LEFT AND RIGHT A black and gold cart creates a sophisticated, even decadent mood for post-prandial drinks. Keep the accessories darkly glamorous, with opulent, glittering glassware and cocktail accoutrements in metallic hues. A handful of dark red ranunculus provides the finishing touch – lush, velvety roses or tulips would make a good substitution.

Zaza

Adding a little French romance to your evening, the darkly glamorous Zaza cocktail is named after an 1898 French play that was made into a film – a rags-to-riches tale of a music hall singer who becomes the mistress and lover of an aristocrat. The strong, sweet taste and rich red shade of the drink will complement the sultry styling of this bar cart.

35 ml/1¼ fl oz. gin

35 ml/1¼ fl oz. Dubonnet

dash of Angostura bitters

a maraschino cherry or orange zest, to garnish

cocktail shaker

barspoon or stirrer

coupe glass

SERVES 1

Fill a cocktail shaker with ice cubes and add the gin, Dubonnet and bitters. Stir well and strain into a chilled coupe glass. Garnish with a maraschino cherry or twist of orange zest and serve immediately.

SCANDI STYLE

SCANDI STYLE

EVEN THE SMALLEST APARTMENT CAN
FIND A NOOK FOR A BAR CART IF IT'S
PETITE AND FOLDABLE.

Essentially a tray on wheels, a simple, pared-down
folding cart like this is perfect for small-space living.
Bring it out when you entertain, and tuck (or fold) it
away when it isn't needed. Place it close to a shelf
or windowsill, and you will immediately increase your
work surface, providing additional room for any extras
that don't fit on the cart. Choose just one or two
cocktails to serve, and display only what's required
for them. This bijou cart has an elegant Scandinavian
feel and has been stocked with sleek modern
glassware that matches the clean lines of the cart.
Add some tumblers for wine and choose larger
pieces – jugs/pitchers, vases – in a unifying finish,
here pale green and ridged. Rather than a sleek
metal shaker, try a large mason/Kilner jar for mixing
drinks. Polished slate coasters and a handmade
bowl for garnishes add a typically Scandi handcrafted
element to the otherwise sleek and refined look.

OPPOSITE AND ABOVE RIGHT If you're short of space, keep your
cart contents to a minimum, with just enough ingredients and glassware
for a couple of chosen drinks. Pretty cocktail napkins are a good way
to introduce more colour and pattern.

OPPOSITE **Aquavit** is just the right fit for a Scandi-themed cart. This Nordic spirit is flavoured with herbs and spices and the dominant flavour is caraway or dill seed. Serve ice cold and garnished with fresh dill for a zesty, botanical tipple that goes perfectly with seafood.

ABOVE Adjacent surfaces such as shelves and pieces of furniture can provide overflow space for additional glassware or an ice bucket. A small cart may not have enough surface area for a vase of flowers, so try to add a colour-coordinated arrangement nearby.

RIGHT Elegant, streamlined aperitif glasses contrast perfectly with the rugged good looks of a handmade carafe.

Homemade Dill Aquavit

Aquavit is a flavoured alcoholic spirit popular in Scandinavia. A jar of the homemade stuff is the perfect authentic addition to your Scandi-style bar cart, both oh-so chic in their simplicity. Dill, caraway and fennel are common flavourings, but berries or flowers can be used too. Purists would use an aquavit base like Brøndums, but vodka is much easier to get hold of outside of Scandinavia.

1 bunch of fresh dill

1 teaspoon caster/ granulated sugar

350 ml/1½ cups vodka, plus extra to taste

large sterilized mason/ Kilner jar and glass bottle

coffee filter

shot glasses

MAKES AROUND 350 ML/12 FL OZ.

Blanch the dill in boiling water for a few seconds, then shake dry and add to the jar (blanching fresh herbs before adding gives a stronger taste). Add the sugar, then top up with vodka and stir. Seal the jar and leave for 5–6 days at room temperature. Strain through a coffee filter to remove the dill. Decant into a bottle and keep for another month before topping up with more vodka to taste. Serve chilled in shot glasses.

RECYCLED
CHIC

RECYCLED CHIC

IN RECENT YEARS THE IDEA OF RECYCLING AND REPURPOSING HAS MADE IT TO THE MAINSTREAM – AT LONG LAST! IF YOU FAVOUR THE WEATHERED, INDUSTRIAL LOOK, THERE ARE A FEW OPTIONS FOR CREATING A CART.

You could fashion your own from reclaimed wood and industrial piping; add wheels to the bottom of a stack of weathered wooden boxes, turned on their side to house your bottles and glassware within; or source an old metal cart like this one at a flea market. Whatever you choose, stick to a palette of natural materials with gently worn finishes. Collect small wooden boxes and trays to organize your glassware, bottles and accessories. Look for recycled glasses, often recognizable thanks to their wobbly and green-tinged finish, or collect pretty jam/preserve jars with rims thin enough to comfortably drink from. For coasters, try small wooden rounds or misshapen pieces of slate or marble – too small for much else, and often discarded. Potted herbs add colour and life, and don't forget to keep scissors handy to snip off sprigs to add to your cocktail or mocktail of choice.

ABOVE AND OPPOSITE The weathered metal finish of this cart from Rockett St George lends itself to a rustic, botanical drinks menu. Fresh herbs soften the recycled styling and are the perfect addition to a non-alcoholic spirit.

OPPOSITE Continue the recycled theme with sturdy green recycled glassware in a variety of different shapes and sizes.

ABOVE LEFT Instead of fruit or flowers, bring your cart to life with fresh herbs to garnish or include in your cocktails. A natural wooden box makes the perfect planter.

ABOVE RIGHT As low and non-alcoholic drinks increase in popularity, why not put together a cart that's bound to appeal to drinkers and non-drinkers alike? Exotic alcohol-free offerings have made it onto the menu of chic cocktail bars around the globe, and more and more drink producers are developing their own no-alcohol libations.

GARDEN 108

Choose an unfussy drink with natural or herbal flavours to go with the rustic, earth-loving theme of your recycled bar cart. Seedlip is a great choice for a grown-up mocktail such as this, infused with hand-picked peas, home-grown hay and garden herbs, it is the world's first distilled non-alcoholic spirit. Perfect served over ice with a full-flavoured and chilled tonic.

50 ml/2 fl oz.
Seedlip Garden 108

120 ml/4 fl oz. tonic water (1724 Tonic Water or Fever-Tree Indian Tonic Water)

fresh lemon thyme sprigs, to garnish

barspoon

gin copa glass

SERVES 1

Add fresh ice cubes to fill ¾ of the glass. Stir gently for 15 seconds with a barspoon to chill the glass. Pour away any liquid from the melted ice. Top up the glass with more ice. Add the gin trying to ensure that you coat the ice as you pour. Add the tonic water. Pouring slowly helps the tonic to keep its fizz. Add your lemon thyme garnish. Let rest for 30 seconds to allow the flavours to integrate before serving.

INDEX

SOURCES

THE CARTS

Graham & Green
grahamandgreen.co.uk
A selection of drinks trolleys, home bars and wine cabinets, including the models seen on pages 39, 47 and 103. Also a huge range of drinkware and tableware perfect for dining and entertaining, including novelty bar accessories, drinks buckets, carafes, jugs and pitchers and decorative napkins.

John Lewis
johnlewis.com
All the bar essentials, from ice trays to bottle openers, as you'd expect. Also a small range of chic carts plus almost every size and shape of glass imaginable.

Oliver Bonas
oliverbonas.com
Gold and marble carts and a slim drinks cabinet that's perfect for small spaces.

Restoration Hardware
restorationhardware.com
Sleek deco chrome and steamer-trunk style carts plus a polyhedron-shaped cart worthy of a Bond villain's lair. Also sophisticated brass cocktail equipment inspired by modernist Italian design.

Rockett St George
rockettstgeorge.com
Quirky accessories – a rocket cocktail shaker and glass drinking straws complete with metal charms – plus a range of different bar carts, including those featured on pages 30, 63, 86, 95 and 119.

The Vintage Trader
thevintagetrader.co.uk
Unique retro bar carts – whatever your style, there'll be a cart to suit you. Also decorative objects, including vintage glassware and brass pineapple ice buckets.

Vinterior
vinterior.co
Independent dealers worldwide offering a selection of fabulous carts, from Hollywood Regency to Danish Modern style.

Westelm
westelm.com
Carts in a range of sizes and finishes plus decorative barware.

GLASSWARE AND ACCESSORIES

Anna Hayman
annahaymandesigns.com
Biba-esque fringed lampshades, as seen on page 103.

Anthropologie
anthropologie.com
Coasters for all carts and all occasions, from woven seagrass styles to sophisticated gold-rimmed geodes. Also decorative glassware, carafes and ceramic pitchers.

Cheekytiki
cheekytiki.com
Ceramic tiki mugs and bamboo cups plus Tiki-inspired decorative accessories and carvings, paper straws and even soft furnishings. Absolutely everything you could need for a tiki party!

Cocktail Kingdom
cocktailkingdom.co.uk
All the kit the home mixologist could need or desire, from matt black cocktail shakers to reusable straws to novelty bar spoons and swizzle sticks. Also a large selection of glassware in all shapes and sizes.

Ecostrawz
ecostrawz.co.uk
Stainless steel, glass and natural bamboo and wheat straws for your cart.

Fishs Eddy
fishseddy.com
Novelty glasses to suit all themes, from politician shot glasses to Moscow mule mugs.

Skandium
skandium.com
Scandinavian glassware from Ittala, Orrefors and Kosta Boda plus the iconic Manhattan cocktail shaker from Georg Jensen and stainless steel ice cooler by Stelton.

Soho Home
sohohome.com
Their glamorous Art Deco-inspired Barwell range includes a martini shaker, ice bucket and cut crystal glassware including champagne coupes.

Tom Dixon
tomdixon.net
The British designer's Plum range includes a futuristic copper-plated shaker plus matching martini glasses, a tray, a mouth-blown glass ice bucket and tongs. Also worth checking out for sleek modern glassware.

Vitrine3
vitrine3.com
Lovingly curated selection of vintage kitchenalia and bar accessories, including glamorous vintage champagne buckets, soda siphons and retro ice buckets like the one shown on page 119.

Viva la Frida
Vivalafrida.co.uk
Papel Picado banners for a Mexican-themed cart.

PICTURE CREDITS

All photography by Cath Gratwicke, apart from the following

Peter Cassidy
Page 114

Addie Chinn
Pages 74, 99

Gavin Kingcome
Pages 23–25

Adrian Lawrence
Pages 17, 107

William Lingwood
Pages 18, 22, 51, 67

Alex Luck
Pages 34, 43, 59, 83, 90, 123, 128

Emma Mitchell
Page 126

Illustrations on pages 20–21 by Selina Snow. Other artworks by

HardtIllustrations/
Shutterstock.com
Pages 36–37, 52–53, 60–61, 76–77, 92–93, 108–109

Mangata/Shutterstock.
com
Pages 44–45, 84–85, 116–117

Picksell/Shutterstock.com
Pages 29–30, 68–69, 100–101

EMILY HENSON is a London-based interior stylist and art director known for her creative and approachable style. After nearly 20 years living in New York and Los Angeles and working as a display artist, merchandiser and stylist, Emily returned home to London where she now styles and art directs photo shoots for clients including Graham & Green, Anthropologie and IKEA. She is the author of four books, *Modern Rustic*, *Bohemian Modern*, *Life Unstyled* and *Be Bold* (all published by Ryland Peters & Small). Emily also hosts talks and workshops on styling and writes a popular blog, Life Unstyled. She has a loyal and growing following on all social media channels @lifeunstyled and lives in London with her two teenage children.

RECIPE CREDITS

Brontë Aurell
Page 114 Homemade Dill Aquavit

Julia Charles
Page 36 Blackberry Bellini
Page 122 Garden 108

Jesse Estes
Page 58 Old Fashioned

Laura Gladwin
Page 34 Aviation Royale
Page 82 Jalisco Flower
Page 106 Zaza

Ben Reed
Pages 9–24
Page 50 Beachcomber's Gold
Pages 66 Mai Tai

David T. Smith
Page 90 Barrel-aged G&T

Tristan Stephenson
Page 74 Singapore Sling
Page 98 Negroni

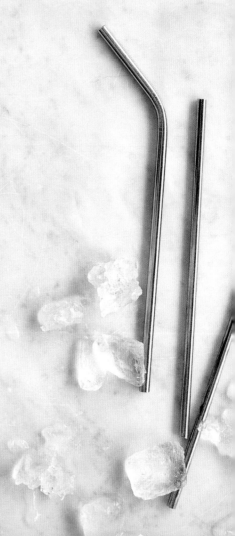